BY VALERIE BODDEN

Published in 2011 by Franklin Watts
338 Euston Road
London NW1 3BH

Franklin Watts Australia
Level 17/207 Kent Street
Sydney NSW 2000

First published by Creative Education
P.O. Box 227, Mankato, Minnesota 56002
Creative Education is an imprint of The Creative Company
www.thecreativecompany.us

ISBN 978 1 4451 0592 5
Dewey number: 915.4'96

Design and production by The Design Lab
Art direction by Rita Marshall

Photographs by 123RF (Dmitry Rukhlenko), Big Stock Photo
(Bobby Singapore), Corbis (Corbis Sygma, Wolfgang Kaehler, Layne
Kennedy, Danny Lehman, Buddy Mays, Reuters, Galen Rowell,
Kevin Schafer, Sea World of California, Nik Wheeler, Staffan
Widstrand), Dreamstime (Sunheyy), iStockphoto (Emre Ogan)

Every attempt has been made to clear copyright. Should there be any
inadvertent omission, please contact the publisher for rectification.

Franklin Watts is a division of Hachette Children's Books,
an Hachette UK company.
www.hachette.co.uk

Printed in China

GREAT PLANET EARTH
MOUNT EVEREST

W
FRANKLIN WATTS
LONDON • SYDNEY

The Himalayas

ASIA

Mount Everest (*EV-er-ist*) is the tallest mountain in the world. It is found in the **continent** of Asia. Half of the mountain is in Nepal. The other half is in an area of China called Tibet. Mount Everest is part of the Himalayan (*him-uh-LAY-en*) mountains.

Mount Everest can be seen from outer space. This image was taken from the Space Shuttle *Atlantis*.

Mount Everest

In Nepal, Mount Everest
is known as Sagarmatha,
or 'goddess of the sky'.

Mount Everest is 8,850 metres tall. That is as high as some planes fly in the sky! Mount Everest has three sides or faces. The sides are shaped like triangles.

Scientist have found that Mount Everest is still growing! Every year, it is believed to grow by about five millimetres.

Section of
Himalayan rock

Mount Everest was formed around 70 million years ago when two huge **plates** of the Earth's **crust** crashed into each other. The collision pushed up great piles of rock which, over millions of years, formed into the Himalayas.

The Himalayas were created when waves of **magma** deep in the Earth's core pushed two plates into each other. Magma sometimes reaches the surface of the Earth through volcanoes (right).

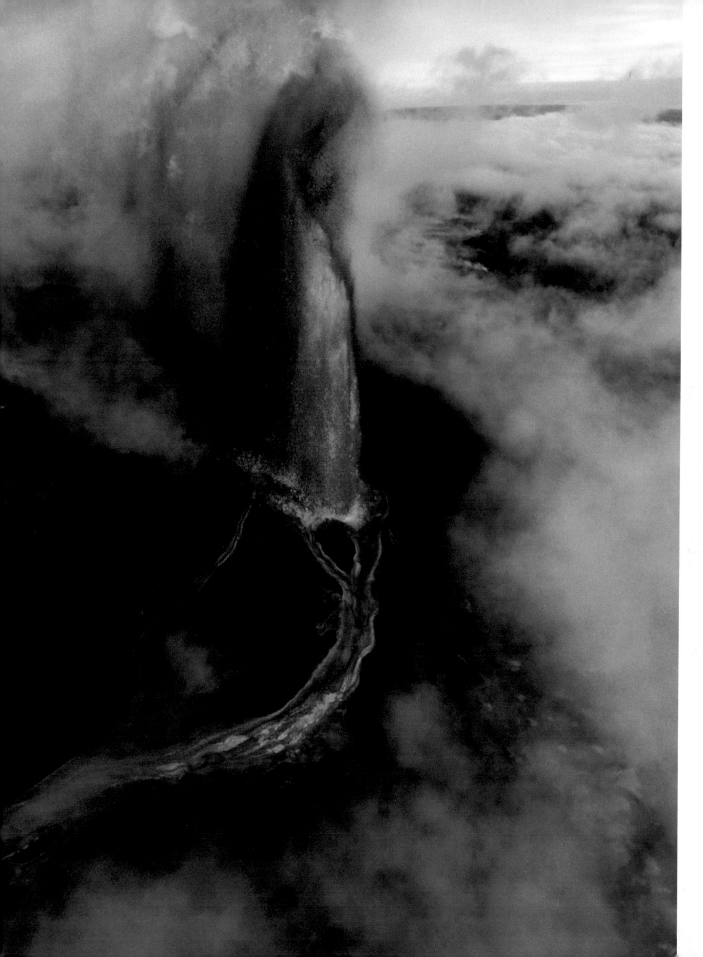

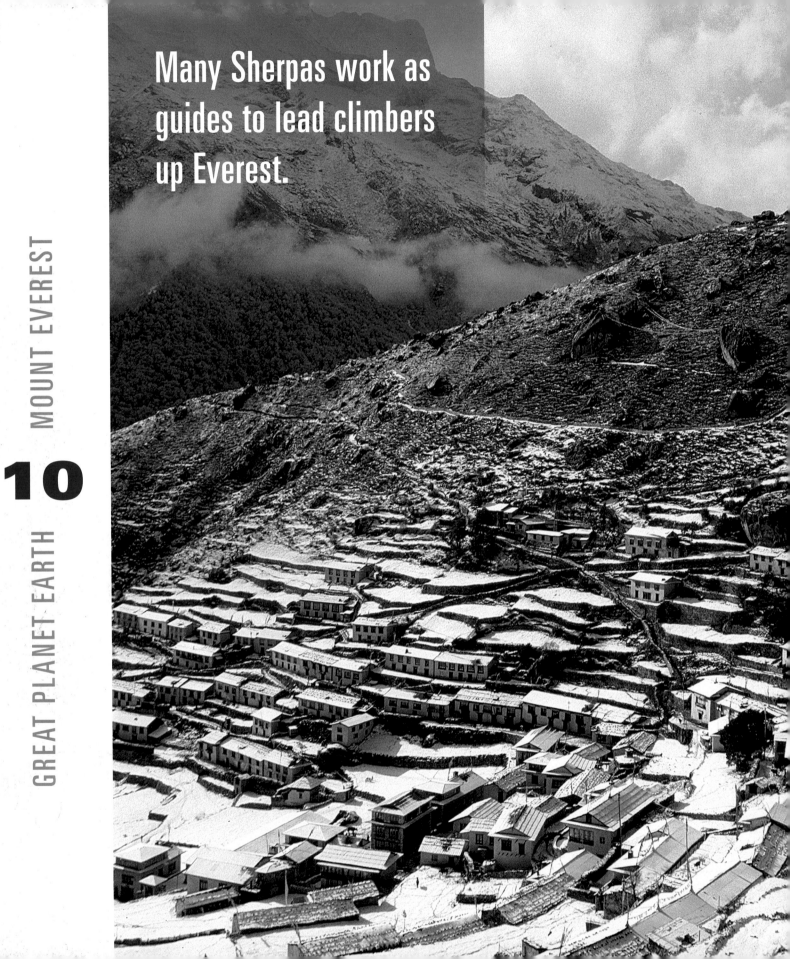

Many Sherpas work as guides to lead climbers up Everest.

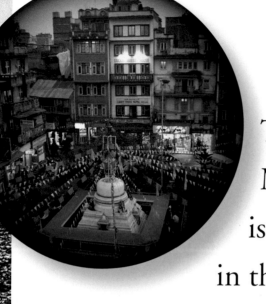

The weather on Mount Everest is very cold, even in the summer. It is covered with snow all year round. People do not live on Mount Everest. But **native** people called Sherpas live in villages close to the bottom of the mountain.

Climbers travel through Sherpa villages in Nepal (left) to reach Mount Everest. The closest city to Mount Everest is Kathmandu (above).

Forests of pine and hemlock trees grow at the bottom of Mount Everest. Animals such as musk deer, pikas (related to hares and rabbits) and Himalayan tahrs (*TARZ*) live in the forests.

Himalayan tahrs (right) are related to wild goats.

Higher up on Mount Everest there are no trees because it is too cold and windy. But there are some small **shrubs**. Snow leopards and mountain sheep can live in these areas. Nothing can survive for long at the very top of Mount Everest.

Snow leopards (left) can survive well on the lower slopes of Everest. Their light-coloured coats help them to blend in with the snow and ice.

It is very difficult and dangerous to climb Mount Everest. On 29 May 1953, climbers Edmund Hillary and Sherpa Tenzing Norgay became the first people to reach the **summit** of Everest. Their climb took many days, but because they had limited **oxygen** they could only stay at the top for 15 minutes!

Edmund Hillary (far left) and Tenzing Norgay (second from left) and the team are greeted as they arrive back from their historic climb.

A Sherpa named Appa has climbed Mount Everest more than 15 times!

GREAT PLANET EARTH

18

MOUNT EVEREST

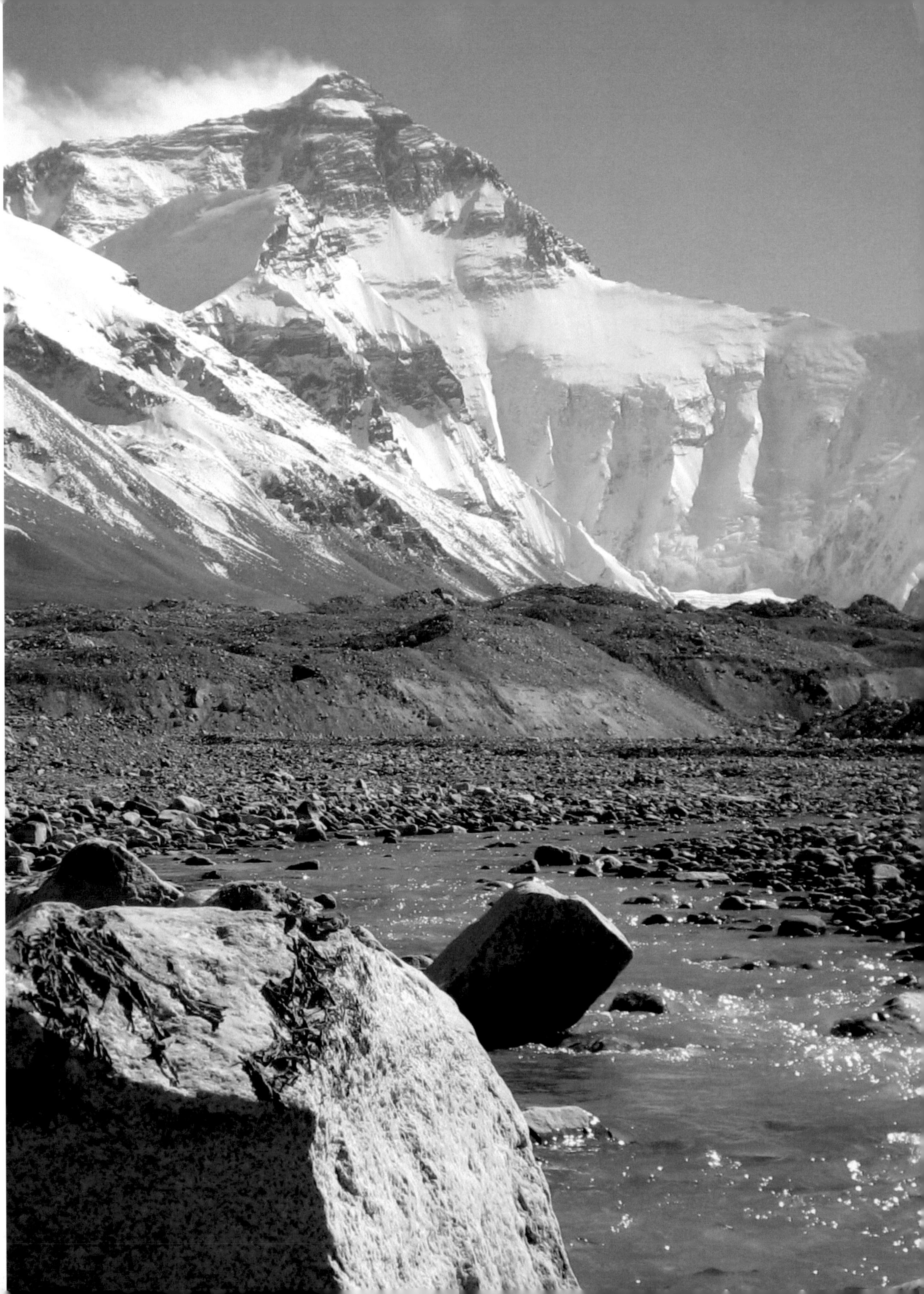

Over the years, many climbers have left rubbish behind on Mount Everest. Some have also cut down trees for firewood. But today, the biggest threat to Everest is **global warming**. Rising temperatures mean that ice and snow on the mountain are melting faster than ever before.

Global warming is making Everest even more dangerous to climb. Climbers are now at risk from **flash flooding** as melting ice and snow pour into local rivers.

Every year, hundreds of people set off to climb Mount Everest. It can take them more than two months to reach the summit. But when they get there, they can enjoy the view from 'the roof of the world'!

A ladder bridge (above) can help climbers reach the top of Mount Everest (right).

Temperatures at the top
of Mount Everest can
drop as low as -73°C.

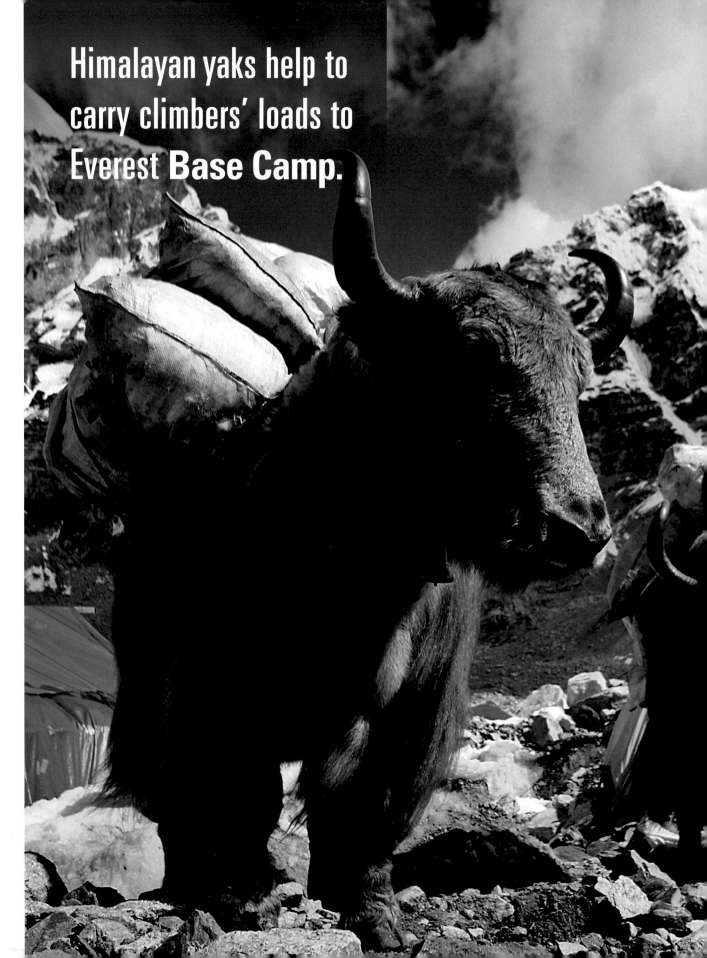

Himalayan yaks help to carry climbers' loads to Everest **Base Camp.**

Glossary

Base Camp a camp next to Everest where climbers rest before beginning their climb

continent one of Earth's seven big pieces of land

crust the solid top layer of the Earth

flash flooding a sudden rush of water

global warming a gradual increase in the Earth's temperature

magma very hot molten rock

native coming from a place

oxygen a gas in the air that people need to breathe to survive

plates separate parts of Earth's crust that move around

shrubs short, woody plants that have many stems

summit the top

Read More about It

Great Journeys Across Earth: Hillary and Norgay's Mount Everest Adventure, (Heinemann, 2008)

Extreme Habitats: Mountains, Susie Hodge (TickTock Books, 2007)

Index